BUSINESS MANAGEMENT

Advanced Level Revision Guide.

SOLOMON MBAIMBAI

TafaPrint

BY SOLOMON .T. MBAIMBAI

+263-773 365 708

Published by:

Tafaprint Publishers
Harare, Zimbabwe
00236-771 318 720

TAFAPRINT

© 2017 Solomon T. Mbaimbai

help@CornerstoneWriters.com

Cover by Tafadzwa Mahachi

ISBN-13: 978-1985046436
ISBN-10: 1985046431

BUSINESS MANAGEMENT

Advanced Level Revision Guide.

CONTENTS

Acknowledgements

First I would like to thank the Almighty, God, for the gift of knowledge he has given me. I would also take this opportunity to thank my family, friends and students for their material and moral support during the writing of the manuscript. I also would like to take this moment to thank Realside College, Creative Partners Private Limited and Mecolite Trading for the financial support they extended towards this project. Finally, I would also want to take this moment to thank various publishers, authors, and professional institutions whose material have provided me with a vast resource of material which I have used in writing this revision guide.

THE FOUNDATION OF EXCELLENCE

Most books just brings a lot of study materials, but This guide recognizes that, sometimes the problem isn't the shortage of material but the shortage of advice on how to use the material, as a solution This guide has taken considerable time to carefully research and **freely** give our valued students the following study and exam passing tips.

1. Manage your study time well

Time is money and eventually money is power, failure to manage time properly may lead to regrets. Your ability to pass will largely depend on how you manage time as a student. Follow the next simple rules for easy time management.

- Make yourself a study schedule. Don't read aimlessly, failing to plan means planning to fail.

- Use piece rate not time rate. Studying is not measured by the amount of time you spend on books but by how many things you have mastered.

- Start out each day with a clear list of things you want to do. Direction is more important than speed.

- Avoid joining unproductive activities or conversations. Your goal to get a Pass is yours alone.

- Review your schedule at the end of the day. Use the Japanese approach of "Kaizen", continuous improvement.

2. Declare war on procrastination

Procrastination is the biggest enemy of success. Declare war on it and destroy it. Always ask yourself "is this the best thing that I could be doing right now?" and if your answer is No! , then change immediately. Always have that voice in your head that says "Go back to work! Go back to studying!" Remember failure knows no excuses, no matter how good your excuses are, failure is just failure so stop procrastination and start **Doing**.

3. Conquer your material

After every lesson, take 5-10 minutes just reviewing what you have learnt , after the whole day try to sit down for a moment just to summarise new things you have learnt all day on a piece of paper.

Going to lessons all day is only helpful if you actually find time to understand what you have learnt. Make sure that you don't do next day's work before you revise the previous day's work. Let the following two rules apply.
- Try to work technical courses such as accounting and mathematics in pairs or groups.

- For theory subjects have discussions with others once or twice a week to see if you are on the right path.

4. Practice! Practice! Practice!

Zimsec or Cambridge, and other exam boards may change the numbers or words but the concepts that are tested are still the same so the best way to prepare for an exam is to revise and understand as many past exam papers and questions as possible. The idea does not lie in cramming the answers but it lies in getting the main concepts that are tested in an exam. A good student does not cram but masters his/her subject, this can only be achieved through practice and more practice. Remember practice makes perfect not cramming.

Before the exam

- Make sure you have encountered a past exam paper of the exam you are writing that day.

- Make sure you know the general time and rule of the paper.

- Arrive at the exam venue 30mins before the exam.

- Bring the required materials only and nothing more.

In the exam

- Always read the instructions of the paper carefully.

- Make a time budget on every question you intend to take on each question.

- Start with the questions that you know well, it will boost your confidence.

- If you run out of time, better answer a few questions very well than to write nothing on many questions.

- Do not panic no matter how difficult the exam is because you make it worse .

"The dictionary is the only place where success comes before work. In real life, by the time you see the results; know that the work has already been done."

BUSINESS AND ITS ENVIRONMENT

1. **State any three different ways in which the size of a business might be measured.** **[3]**

- Number of employees; Market share; Sales turnover; Total profits; Capital employed; Number of Branches.

2. **Outline any four methods of de-Integration** **[4]**

- Demerger; Divestment; Management buyout; Management buy in; Sub-contracting.

3. **What is meant by the term quota** **[2]**

- It is a trade restriction whereby the government puts a physical limit on the number of units an individual can import, e.g. if importing shoes or clothes from Botswana, duty free is limited to four units per product, any excess will be charged duty.

4. **Why the government of your country may be worried about increased import expenditure [4].**

- Leads to balance of payment deficit.
- Affects survival and growth of domestic firms producing similar goods.
- Adversely affect terms of trade.
- Contribute to shortage of foreign currency.
- Lead to depreciation of local currency.

5. **Why are most governments keen to promote exports [4]**

- In order to improve the balance of payment
- Exports stimulate economic growth
- In order to reduce unemployment as exporting firms employ more people to increase output
- To enhance economic relations with other trading economies.

6. **Distinguish between internal and external constraints on businesses.   [2]**

- Internal constraints refers to environmental variables that management can control e.g. workforce, managerial skills etc. whereas external environment refers to environmental variable beyond the control of the business e.g. government policies, inflation, unemployment etc.

7. **Explain three difficulties faced by small firms in their operations   [6**

- Lack of capital--small firms find it difficult to raise finance due to lack of collateral security, this makes their expansion difficult.
- Lack of expertise--due to limited financial resources small firms do not afford to employ high calibre staff with expertise to manage their business effectively.

- Suffer from stiff competition from large firms which result in a low sales turnover as well as profitability.
- Do not enjoy economies of scale--these results in cost disadvantages as they incur high cost per unit as fixed cost are spread over a small volume of output.
- Lack of suitable premises as most strategic locations are expensive beyond the reach of small firms e.g. office space in the CBD are expensive.
- Lack of continuity if the owner dies, as most of business strategies rely on the well being of the owner hence the owner's death may lead to collapse of the business.

8. State and explain three ways in which the government can offer assistance to small firm. [6]

- Government can offer low interest loans to small firms so as to provide the needed finance to expand their businesses.
- Government can offer small firms grants and subsidies so as to reduce their cost of production there by making their products competitive in the market.
- Government can offer training to small firms in order to increase their expertise through government organized workshops and seminars.
- Government can build factory shells for small firms and rent them at affordable rents.
- Government can put import restrictions in order to protect local small firms from cheap imports.

9. Justify the need for growth of firms in your country. [4]

The growth of firms in my country is of vital importance as it may lead to:
- Increase in GDP
- Employment creation
- Improvement in the standard of living
- Increased revenue for the government

10. State any four objectives of businesses in your country.   [4]

Profit maximization; Growth; Survival; Social responsibility; Sales maximization

11. Giving examples, distinguish between stakeholders and shareholders.   [4]

- Stakeholders refers to any individual with an interest in the operations of a business e.g. customers, suppliers etc whereas shareholders are investors of the company who have contributed capital e.g. ordinary shareholders.
- The main objective of stakeholders is survival of the firm whereas the main objective of shareholders is profit maximization.

12. State any six stakeholders of a business.   [6]

- Employees; Shareholders; Management; Government; Suppliers; Community; Competitors.

13. State any two levels of economic activity.   [2]
- Primary sector;   Secondary sector; Tertiary sector.

14. Why might goods and services be provided by the public sector in your country? [4]

- In order to provide essential services at affordable prices.
- To control natural monopolies and prevent exploitation of the public by profit seeking firms.
- To correct market failure by providing goods and services left by private sector.
- To control strategic industries such as defence, electricity generation.
- Some industries require large capital investment which private individuals cannot raise hence should be provided by the state which has capacity to raise such capital.

15. Distinguish between public limited and private limited companies. [4]

Public limited company	Private limited company
Issue shares to the public	Issue of shares is restricted to directors
Members range from 2 to infinite	Members range from 1-50
Name ends with plc	Name ends with pvt ltd
Business affairs are public	Business affairs are private
Company secretary must be qualified	Company Secretary may or may not be qualified

16. State three reasons for going private.   [3]

- In order for the shareholders to retain full control of the firm.
- To reduce threats of takeover.
- To run away from cost associated with stock exchange listing.

17. State any two examples of economic systems. [2]

- Free market enterprise;   Command economy; Mixed economy.

18. What do you understand by the term legal personality? [3]

- It is a status that defines a company as a separate legal entity from its owners. The company runs itself as a limited company and it can sue or be sued.

19. Explain the importance of legal personality to a business organisation.   [4]

- Allows the business to own property in its own name.
- The owner's personal misfortunes will not affect business performance.
- Ensures business continuity as death of one shareholder will not disrupt business performance.
- Allows business to raise more capital as investors risk is reduced due to limited liability.

20. Define the term inflation.   [2]

- It is a sharp increase in the general price levels, which will result in too much money chasing few goods.

21. Explain the effects of inflation on businesses. [4]

Aggregate demand will shrink as money loses its purchasing power leading to reduced profitability for firms. High inflation makes planning for firms difficult due to excessive fluctuations of prices. It also leads to an increase in production cost as workers bargain for high wages. However high inflation benefits a firm if it has fixed interest debt capital (High gearing) as it benefits from paying low interest. Also a firm benefits from increasing value of stock.

22. Explain how the government's monetary policy affects businesses in your country. [4]

- Government uses monetary policy to control the economy through interest rates and money supply. If the monetary policy is contraction, firms will realize a fall in demand, sales and profits due to decreased expenditure as money supply decreases and interest rates increases. **However** if the monetary policy is expansionary firms will realize an increase in demand, sales and profit levels due to an increase in consumer expenditure as a result of an increase in money supply and a decrease in the cost of borrowing (interest rates).

23. Outline any four benefits of technological improvement to businesses in your country [4]

- Increases the level of productivity due to increased efficiency.
- Reduces labour cost as machines will replace labour
- Increased convenience and customer service e.g. the use of ATMs in banks
- Simplifies work thus making it easier to perform.

24. State any three legal constraints that affect businesses operations.   [3]

- laws restricting mergers
- laws restricting freedom of advertising
- laws restricting on financial structure
- price controls

25. State any three types of business culture.   [3]

- Task culture;   Person culture; Power culture; Bureaucratic culture; Adventurous culture

26. Outline any four factors that influence corporate culture.

- History of the organisation; Structure of the organisation; Technological change; Size of the organisation; Management philosophy; External factors e.g. political environment.

27. Discuss the importance of management by objectives [5]

MBO motivates subordinates by providing a sense of belonging due to a high degree of involvement and participation. Secondly it enhances communication as there is frequency of interaction between managers and subordinates. It leads to increased commitment and job satisfaction as people thrive more to achieve targets they have set for themselves. **However, MBO** consumes time due to consultations in decision making. It also results in increased paper work due to frequency of meetings. Despite the drawbacks of MBO, managers should embrace MBO as an aid to effective management so as to increase managerial efficiency.

28. Using examples, distinguish between vertical and lateral integration. [4]

Vertical integration	Lateral integration
Merger of firms in different stages of production	Merger of firm in similar stage of production but Offering products that do not compete directly with each other
e.g. a bakery merge with a wheat farmer	e.g. a furniture retailer merge with a clothes retailer
Firms do not use similar production techniques	Firms use similar production techniques.

29. How are businesses affected by an increase in taxation?

- Reduces profits available for reinvestment thus hindering growth
- Raises prices of goods leading to contraction of demand which will in turn reduce sales and profits of firms.
- Reduces consumer spending by reducing their disposable income.

30. Outline any three drawbacks of import controls. [3]

- Reduces variety in the economy which will lead to reduced consumer choice.
- It may result in retaliation by other countries which may have a negative impact on the export market.
- May promote inefficiencies by local firms due to reduced competition.
- May reduce living standards.

31. Why may the government of your country limit the entry of multinational companies in the country? [4]

- MNCs may interfere in local politics
- MNCs Repatriate profits to their mother country
- Exploitation of natural resources which may result in the depletion of non renewable resources.
- Exploitation of labour as the pay low wage rates in host country compared to the wage rates in their mother country.

- May stifle growth of local firms through stiff competition.

32. **Explain the influence of any two elements of macro environment to a business of your choice. [4]**

   - Unemployment-high unemployment reduces demand as individuals are starved of income, this will result in reduced sales and profitability for firms, and however it may benefit firms through reduced wage rates as supply of labour increases.
   - TAX-high taxes erodes the firms profit thus hindering its potential for internal growth, however it may result in increased public expenditure which may drive economic growth, which will in turn result in increased opportunities for firms.
   - Interest rates- high interest rates will hinder growth of firms as cost of borrowing increases, conversely low interest rates facilitates growth as borrowing becomes cheap.

33. **Explain the importance of limited liability to shareholders. [3]**

- It reduces shareholders risk by limiting their liability to what they have only invested in the business. It also prevents the misfortunes of an individual shareholder from affecting the business and other shareholders' interest.

34. State any three features of public limited companies. [3]

- Issue shares to the public.
- It is obliged to provide financial statements to the public through the press.
- Name ends with plc.
- Must employ a qualified secretary.

35. What is the importance of small business operations in your country? [5]

- Create more job opportunities, thus helping to reduce unemployment.
- Increase competition which will result in quality products at low prices.
- Widen government revenue base as small firms pay taxes to the central government and license fees to the local government.
- Fill gaps left by large firms.
- Play a supportive role to large firms through the provision of components and services that large firm cannot provide on their own.

36. Explain the reasons why some firms remain small. [6]

- Owners fear losing control of the business.
- Growth may lead to diseconomies of scale.
- Limited capital
- Desire to maintain privacy of business information.

37. Why is it important for businesses to plan?   [4]

Planning is important for businesses as it:
- Provide a sense of direction.
- help in prioritizing activities
- enhances coordination
- enhance delegation.
- act as a tool of motivating workers if they were involved in the planning process.

38. Explain any three ethical constraints.   [6]

- Tribalism
- corruption
- Cultural barriers.
- Patronage
-

N.B. emphasis should be on explaining the points.

39. Identify any three objectives of an economy [3]

- Economic growth
- Reduce unemployment
- Low inflation
- Balance of payment equilibrium.
- Reduce public debt.

40. Explain why new businesses fail.   [4]

- Poor planning
- Lack of working capital.
- Poor managerial skills.
- Stiff competition from existing firms.

41. Define the term demerger. [2]

- It is the creation of two or more quoted companies from one existing company for example the splitting of ZESA into ZETDC, ZPS and REA

42. Define the term divestment. [2]

- It is a process of reducing the scope of activities of a business by selling some of its subsidiary companies.

43. How may macro-economic policies of government affect business objectives and strategies? [4]

The answer should explain the ways in which government policies can influence business objectives and strategies at large. The policies to be explained include:
- Interest rates
- Taxation
- Exchange rates
- Import controls
- Government expenditure
- Government incentives to industries e.g. grants and subsidies

PEOPLE IN ORGANISATION

1. WHAT IS AN ORGANISATION CHART? [2]

Question requires a simple definition of an organization chart.

-It is a pictorial or a diagrammatic representation of functions, departments, structures and people in an organization.

-It is a pictorial representation of the formal framework that shows how authority is passed or is flowing in an organization.

-It is a diagrammatic representation of relationships in an organization that explains how roles, authority and responsibilities are shared among members of the organisation.

2. Explain two reasons why an organisational chart would be useful to the employees of a business. [4]

Students are expected to explain fully 2 advantages of organizational charts to employees.

An organizational chart helps people to:

-Set their position in an organization.

-Appreciate their responsibility.

-See who has authority over them and to whom they are accountable to.

-Enables employees to see carrier paths or promotional leaders.

-To know channels of communication.

NB: .One developed reason two marks.

3. What are the results or consequences of poor organisational structures [6?]

-Low motivation and morale.

-Lack of co-ordination and control.

-Poor communication.

-Confusion due to unclear chain of command.

-Duplication of activities which maybe a waste of resources.

-In-effective decision making.

-Divisiveness and lack of co-operation.

4. Distinguish between Douglas McGregor's theory x and y [4]

-Theory X assumes that an average human being has an inherent dislike of work whereas theory Y assumes that workers view work as natural as play or rest.

-According to theory X, human beings avoid responsibility however possible but theory Y states that, under normal circumstances, a human being does not only accept responsibility, but seeks extra responsibility.

-Theory X assumes that human beings must be directed, controlled and even threatened whereas theory Y assumes that a normal human being can exercise self direction and control in the service of the objectives one is committed to.

-Theory X assumes that an average human being is not ambitious whereas theory Y assumes that a normal human being is motivated by ambition.

-Theory X is a pessimistic view of workforce whereas theory Y is an optimistic view of the workforce.

5. How might the differences in McGregor's theory x and theory y reflected (shown) in the leadership style of a manager [4]

Theory X is normally revealed through:

-Autocratic style of leadership; No delegation; One way communication; Centralization of decision making; Threats and punishment.

Theory Y is normally revealed through:

-Democratic style of leadership; Delegation; Two-way communication; Decentralization of decision making; Consultation and Participation.

6. What are the characteristics of tall structures [4?]

-Decentralized authority.

-Many levels of authority.

-Narrow span of control.

-High level of delegation.

-High degree of functional specialization.

7. State and explain any two reasons for high labour turnover in an organisation [4]

Students are expected to explain only two reasons

-Poor working conditions

-Meager salaries and wages

Poor management style

-Lack of job security

-Lack of status

-Poor relationships with subordinates, peers, superior etc

-Poor motivation

-Unfavorable leadership styles.

8. What is an autocratic leadership style? [2]

-This is a leadership style where a manager has maximum authority and expects unquestioned obedience from subordinates. The manager is highly directive and authoritative and subordinates have minimum freedom as they are expected to follow instructions religiously.

9. Explain the circumstances in which an autocratic management style may be appropriate. [4]

-Where individuals work best under directions and control.

-Where there is no real time for consultation e.g. in a crisis.

-Where disciplinary measures must be observed e.g. Army.

Where danger, difficulty and other problems are common.

-Where the task is structured.

-Where leader has all the information and knowledge to make decision.

10. How useful is oral communication in an organisation [4]

Oral organization may be of great importance to an organization because of the following:

-Can be varied to suite the need of the receiver.

-Can be quickly questioned or queried by the receiver.

-Enhanced by gestures (supported by non verbal cues).

-Allows immediate/spontaneous feedback.

However oral communication has been dismissed on the following grounds:

-There is need to listen carefully.

-Affected by physical noise.

-No permanent and accurate record.

-Can be quickly forgotten.

-Can be affected by distance.

11. Explain any three communication problems that lie with the receiver [6]

Focus should be given in explaining the problems

-Poor listening techniques or habits.

-Emotional barriers.

- Different perception.

-Evaluating the source.

-Hearing what you want to hear.

12. What are the results of communication failure [5]

-Poor decision making.

-High conflicts.

-Poor delegation of tasks.

-Failure to implement plans.

-Mistakes may arise.

13. Explain the factors which influence the choice of appropriate media in communication. [6]

Candidates should fully explain each factor

-Importance of the message to be communicated.

-Speed of information.

-Quantity (size) of data to be communicated.

-The cost involved.

-The advantages to be gained from staff input.

14. **Outline any three forms of communication [4]**

-Oral communication.

-Electronic communication.

-Written communication.

15. **Assess the usefulness of email in communication [4]**

Benefits

-Provides cheap and efficient long distance communication.

-Offer unlimited potential for personal networking.

-Is democratic and open.

Drawbacks

-Subject to information overload.

-Employees can waste valuable time surfing the net.

-It includes incomplete, illegal and trivial information e.g. SPAM

16. What is meant by the term expert power? [2]

-This is power possessed by an individual because of special skills he/she possess for example a doctor has expert power over a patient.

17. What are the advantages and disadvantages of centralisation? [6]

ADVANTAGES	DISADVANTAGES
-Fosters greater control.	-May lead to rigidity.
-Facilitates easier communication	-Leads to excessive bureaucratic.
-Leads to economies of staffing.	-may cause delays in decision making.
	-Stifles personal development.

18. What practices may be used in job enrichment [3]

-Encouraging workers participation.

-Increasing the responsibility of individual workers.

-Provide greater autonomy and responsibility.

-Allowing workers to increase their expertise.

-Provide workers with information.

-Giving people a complete unit of work.

19. Give any three reasons why informal communication channels are important in an organisation [3]

-Satisfy personal needs.

-Counter monotony at work.

-Provide a source of job related information that is not provided by formal channels.

- Spread information fast as it penetrates the tightest security and follows no procedures.

20. Explain what you understand by the term exploitative-authoritative system in leadership [3]

- It is a boss centered approach to leadership were the leader makes all decisions with no room for subordinate participation and it is characterized by one way communication, imposed decisions, threats and the use of coercive power.

21."Workers are solely motivated by financial rewards "Discuss [6]

Student should assess the extent where financial rewards motivate and also highlight the value of non financial rewards. Answer should be supported by relevant theories.

FINANCIAL REWARDS REWARDS	NON- FINANCIAL
-Salary redesign	-Job design and
-Performance related bonuses	-Training
-Price rate	-Job enlargement
-Time rate	- Job enrichment
-Fringe benefits	-Worker participation e.g. MBO

*therefore workers are motivated by a fusion of both financial and non-financial rewards.

22. How does the employer ensure health and safety of workers in an organisation? [3]

-Ensure health and safety measures are adequate.

-Regular checks on maintenance of equipment.

-Offering protective clothing like safety shoes, work suits.

-Training employees in safety issues.

-HIV/AIDS workshops.

-Provision of clinics at organizations.

-Medical aid fund.

-Counseling of employees.

-Mark danger points e.g. "beware of forklifts" or "move slowly-slippery floor ahead".

23. Give any four examples of functional managers [4]

Operations manager; Marketing manager; financial manager; Human resource manager; I T manager.

24. Explain the factors which influence the choice of the leadership style. [4]

Candidates should explain the following factors:

-The nature / demand of the job.

-Organizational culture.

-Expectations of superiors.

-The leader's past experience and expectations.

-Behavior of subordinates.

25. Define the following terms:

a. Job enlargement (horizontal work load) [2]

-It is the horizontal extension of a job which involves redesigning of the job by increasing more tasks, so that the senses of ranks are combined into a new broader job that gives variety of challenges to employees.

b. Job enrichment (vertical work load) [2]

-This is the vertical extension of a job which involves adding both task and responsibility to a job.

26. **Define horizontal communication [3]**

-This refers to communication which takes place between members of the same level in the organization for instance communication between line managers of two or more departments.

27. What is the importance of horizontal communication [4]

-Co-ordinate activities.

-To solve problems.

-To offer choice.

-To share resources such as information.

28. **Explain any two advantages of informal groups to organisations [4]**

-They facilitate fast communication through grape vine.

-They may influence each other positively to work towards organizational goals.

-They provide social satisfaction thus meeting need for affiliation for their members.

-A sense of security is achieved by the feeling of "strength in numbers" of a group.

-They help members to solve their personal problems thus reducing stress.

29. Give any four disadvantages of informal groups to organisations [4]

-May lead to resistance to change.

-Employees will suffer from conformity thus lacking creativity.

-May cause conflicts between management and employees due differing objectives between group and organizational goals.

-Grapevine might spread wrong and harmful information.

30. Is a functional structure always a good structure? [6]

Benefits

-It provides a clear task assignment and trained individuals will find the job that they are interested in.

-Members within departments can easily communicate.

-It provides a very suitable environment for new managers.

-Supervision may become easier.

-Provide a clear career path for personal development.

However, functional structure has the following problems:

-Staff may develop a narrow outlook and will be unable to see the business as a whole.

-It may be difficult to prepare managers for a wide range of functions since there is specialization.

-It can be difficult to make quick decisions since functional managers will have to report to central headquarters.

-It is often difficult to determine accountability and judge performance in functional structure.

31. Explain the advantages and disadvantages of a matrix organisation structure [6]

Advantages

-It allows communication between departments.

-Efforts are channeled towards what is good for the project instead of a department leading to greater commitment.

-The system responds quickly to changing market conditions as teams can be created easily when wanted and also quickly dissolved

Disadvantages

-There is less direct control from the top as teams may be empowered to undertake and complete projects.

-More time will be spent on discussion rather than action.

-Contravenes principle of unity of command as subordinate might still receive instructions from both functional manager and project manager.

32. Explain any four forms of authority [4]

-Formal authority

-Line authority

-Staff authority

-Functional authority

33. Define the following terms

a. **Decentralization** [2]

-This refers to the dispersal or diffusion of decision making authority to the periphery.

b. **Centralisation [2]**

-It is relatively high degree of concentration of decision making authority among very few top level managers.

34. Explain any three variables affecting decentralization. [6]

Students should explain any three of the following factors:

-cost of decision;   -desire for uniformity;   -Size of the organization;   -Diversity of product lines; -Geographical location of the business;   -Type of organizational function; -Philosophy of top managers.

35. Assess the usefulness of decentralization to an organisation [4]

Question should be written in continuous prose

Benefits

-Leads to better decision making as decisions are made where the action is.

-It offers training for junior managers and prepares them for promotion.

-quick response to changes in the market.

-Increase employee motivation through participation in decision making.

Problems

-Co-ordination by top managers may be difficult as organisation hierarchy becomes tall.

-May lead to loss of control by top level managers thus narrowing their view of the organisation.

- may lead to inconsistencies and non uniform decisions.

-Subordinates may pursue their own objectives at the expense of corporate goals.

36. Define the following terms.

a. **Authority [2]**

-It is the capacity of a superior derived from his/her formal position to make decisions that affect the behavior of subordinates.

b. **Unit of command [2]**

-It is a principle which state that every subordinate should report to only one manager to reduce conflicts and confusion.

c. Chain of command [2]

-It is a plan that specifies who reports to who in the organization.

d. Span of control

-It refers to the number of subordinates reporting directly to one superior that is the subordinates to superior ratio.

37. Distinguish between wide and narrow span of control [4]

Narrow span of control	Wide span of control
It is when a manager has a few numbers of subordinates who directly report to them.	It is when a manager have a large number of subordinates who are directly under his supervision.
Leads to a tall organizational structure	Leads to a flat organizational structure
There are high administration cost due to a high number of managers	There are low administration cost due to a few number of managers

38. Give the advantages and disadvantages of wide span of control [4]

Advantages

-Subordinates have greater freedom to exercise their initiatives.

-facilitates delegation.

-Reduced administration costs due to fewer management levels

Disadvantages

-Limited interaction between the manager and subordinates may reduce morale of subordinates.

-Subordinates may abuse their freedom arising from less managerial supervision.

-It over burdens key people thus reducing effectiveness in performance.

39. Explain any three factors affecting span of control [6]

Student should explain the factors fully

-The competence of the manager.

-The knowledge and experience of subordinates.

-Geographical dispersal of subordinates

-The cost of mistakes.

40. What is meant by the term delegation [3?]

-It is the act of assigning formal authority for the completion of specific activities to a subordinate; however ultimate responsibility lies with the manager. It is a process whereby a manager transfers part of the legitimate power to subordinates so as to allow them to par take a high level task on their behalf.

41. Give any three reasons for delegation [3]

-It results in increased participation by subordinates thereby motivating them.

-It relieves managers of less important routine and less immediate tasks to concentrate on more important issues.

-It enables decision to be taken where the action is.

-It trains subordinates to make decisions and prepare them for promotion.

-It provides flexibility by enabling decision making to be done at grass roots level.

42. Give reasons why it is often difficult for managers to effectively delegate work to their subordinates [4]

-Lack of delegation skills.

-Fear that subordinates can perform better than managers.

-Shyness.

-Some managers are power hungry.

43. How can you overcome poor motivation in an organisation [5?]

-Improving conditions of work.

-Offering fringe benefits e.g. transport, subsidized food, education facilities.

-Improving the levels of pay relative to those offered by firms in the same industry.

-Changing to a democratic leadership style.

-Introduction of worker involvement and participation schemes.

- Job designing

-Training

45. What did Maslow meant by self actualisation needs [2]

-These are needs for personal growth by realizing one's full potential.

46. Why is effective communication important in a business? [5]

-Results in quality decision making.

-A source of motivation for the staff.

-May result in effective co-ordination between departments.

-May result in improved problem solving.

-Facilitates speed of reaction to changes in the market.

-It ensures a business to become open and interacts with all its stakeholders.

-Reduces errors and mistakes as information is clearly shared and understood.

47. a. Give any four potential human problems associated with computer use for communication [4]

-Hacking / insecurity.

-Alienation.

-Stress from lack of human contact.

-Illness associated with being too long at the computer.

-Illiteracy.

b. How can these problems are minimized [3]

-Regular staff meeting.

-Training.

-Effective induction.

-Warning devices to alert users to messages.

-Restriction of use to appropriate situations.

48. What are the advantages and disadvantages of using computers in an organisation [6]

Advantages

-They process data much faster than using manual.

-They are able to handle vast quantities of data.

-They are extremely accurate.

-They reduce staff cost as fewer people are needed to operate computers.

Disadvantages

-Installation and setup costs are very high.

-It needs effective training which may be expensive.

-Once a system is designed and installed it may be difficult to change or modify it.

49. Give reasons why motivation of workers is of great importance to the organisation [3]

-It increases productivity.

-It improves quality of the products.

-It retains workers.

-It reduces labor turnover.

-It reduces the errors and mistakes.

50. State three reasons why managers often find it very difficult to effectively communicate with the work force [3]

-Emotional barriers to communication.

-Evaluation of the destination or source of the message.

-Poor listening skills

-Different perception

-Poor organizational structure.

-Lack of will to communicate.

51. Distinguish between authority and responsibility [4]

-Authority is the right to exercise power or to give orders whereas responsibility is an obligation or commitment to carry out a task in accordance with instructions received.

-Authority can be delegated while ultimate responsibility cannot be delegated.

52. What is the difference between job evaluation and performance evaluation [2]

-Job evaluation refers to the relative comparison of the worthiness of the job in relation to other jobs in the organization whereas Performance evaluation is the systemic evaluation of employee performance by comparing actual performance with the expected performance.

53. Give the differences between Personnel and Human resource Management [4]

PERSONNEL MANAGEMENT	HUMAN RESOURCES MANAGEMENT.
-Quantitative in nature	-Qualitative in nature
-Grievances of employees are solved through the worker committees	-Grievances of employees are solved through the trade unions'
-View workers as liabilities.	-View workers as assets

54. Explain any three factors which affect recruitment and selection. [6]

Candidates should explain any three of the following factors:

-Labor market analysis.

-Objectives of the organization.

-Policy of the organization.

-Urgency of the vacancy.

-Government policy on the recruitment.

-Nature of the job.

55. "Organisational conflicts are not always'. What might be the possible benefits of conflicts? [4]

-It strengthens the relationship between employees and management.

-It airs the grievances of the employees.

-It brings out hidden agendas.

-It strengthens the organization.

56. Draw up a job description for a personnel officer[6]

Vacant post: Personnel Officer.

DUTIES AND RESPONSIBILITIES.

-Maintaining employer records up to date.

-Processing the salaries of workers.

-Attending disciplinary hearing.

-Carrying out a salary surveys.

-Preparing job descriptions for various employees.

-Recruitment and selection of employees.

-Designing , implementing and revaluating training.

57. Briefly explain any three managerial functions. [6]

Candidates should explain three from the following functions:

- Planning- It is an ongoing process of pre-determining what to do and how to do it. This means that managers think through their goals and actions in advance.
- Organising- It is a process of arranging and allocating work, authority and resources among

the organisation's members so that they can achieve the organisational goals. It includes staffing and sourcing of funds and materials.

- Leading- This involves directing, influencing and motivating employees to perform essential task efficiently and effectively.
- Controlling- This is a process of ensuring that actual activity conforms to the planned activity. It involves monitoring and checking to see if plans have been truly carried out and taking corrective action if deviations are detected.

58. **Give advantages and disadvantages piece rate as a payment system. [4]**

Advantages

-There is link between output and effort.

-It encourages greater output and a faster pace at work.

Disadvantages

-Lead to reduced quality

-Provides little security over pay

59. **Give reasons why government intervenes in relationship between employees and employers. [4]**

-To settle disputes.

-Provision of safety to employees.

-Observation of worker's rights.

-To provide a sound industrial relations.

60. What is the importance of medical examinations. [3]

-To reject those whose physical qualifications are insufficient to meet the requirements of the job.

-To obtain the record of physical condition of the applicant at the time of hiring.

-To prevent the employment of those with contagious diseases.

-To place those who are otherwise employable but whose physical condition requires assignment to specific duties.

-To protect the firm from unjustified claims of compensation.

61. What are the characteristics of successful leaders. [4]

-Adaptable to situations, (flexible).

-Ambitious and achievement oriented.

-Persistent.

- Good communication skills.

-Co-operative.

-Creative,

-Social skills and self discipline.

62. Circumstances under which employees can be dismissed instantly. [4]

-Misconduct

-Incapacitation

-Theft

-Divulging business privacy to the competitor

-Gross negligence

-incompetence

63. Justify the need for induction training in an organisation. [4]

Students should focus on the advantages of induction training and explain them.

Importance include

-Facilitates easy adjustment to organization culture.

-Less chances of rule violation.

-Employees gain a sense of belonging or feel accepted.

-Boost employee's attitudes towards the organization.

-Reduces labor turnover.

-Reduces accidents, and mistakes.

64. State any two communication methods[2]

-Oral communication.

-Pictorial communication.

-Written communication.

65. Explain what Maslow meant by self actualisation and why he placed it at the top of his pyramid. [3]

The question requires a description of self actualisation and an explanation of why it is at the top of the pyramid.

-Feeling of fulfillment.

-Realizing one's full potential.

-Achievement/accomplishment.

-Personal growth.

-It is placed at the top because such needs are never completely satisfied.

66. Explain any three barriers to effective communication. [6]

Candidates should explain any three of these barriers.

-Perceptual difficulties.

-Use of specialized jargon.

-Technological systems failure.

- Physical noise, (noisy environment).

67. Explain how these barriers in (66) affect business communication. [6]

Effects to be clearly explained are:

-Low morale.

-Un-informed decisions.

-Poor quality work.

-Conflicts.

-Mistakes.

-Lack of co-ordination and control.

68. a) What is meant by the term performance appraisal? [2]

-It is the systematic evaluation of an individual's performance by comparing expected performance with actual performance.

b). Explain the importance of performance appraisal. [4]

Candidates should explain the following terms:

-Gives employees feedback on their performance.

-Provide implementation for making decisions.

-Used for making salary decisions (performance related).

-Forum for guidance and counseling.

-Assessment of employee's potential.

-Need for training identification.

69. Discuss the contribution that informal groups might make towards the overall performance of an organisation. [5]

Positive

-Social satisfaction.

-Fosters better problem solving.

-Improves communication.

-May influence each other positively for organisational progress.

Negative

-Grapevine may spread wrong and harmful rumors.

-They are a strong source of resistance to change.

-May lead to conflict of interest.

-Result in excess conformity.

70. Why is conflict inevitable in a large organisation. [4]

-The need to share scarce resources.

-Workflow interdependence.

-Differences in goals between organization and workers.

-Ambiguously defined responsibility.

-Different perception.

71. What might be the possible benefits of workgroup conflicts? [4]

-Bring hidden issues to the surface.

-Encourages creativity and innovation.

-Enhance communication.

-Increase cohesion of a group when directed to an external agent.

72. Explain the importance of training to an organization. [6]

Candidates should explain the following importance:

-It provides focus and a sense of direction.

-Helps in prioritizing activities.

-It facilitates delegation.

-It forces managers to change.

-Co-ordinates activities.

73. What is training programme?[2]

-Is an organized process designed to maintain or improve current job performance by impacting individuals with skills and knowledge pertaining to a particular job.

74. Why may fear lead to resistance to change?[4]

Students should highlight various types of fear that lead to resistance to change.

-Fear of the unknown.

-Fear of losing the job.

-Fear of losing power, status.

-Fear of losing friends

-Fear of failing to cope up with change

-Fear of losing status

75. Explain any three types of authority. [6]

-Staff authority.

-Line authority.

-Functional authority

76. Why might a firm employ party time workers? [3]

-To match staffing levels to demand.

-To retain valued staff.

-To reduce wage and non wage costs.

-They have fewer statutory rights.

-Workers are less likely to be unionized.

-To perform tasks for which there is insufficient need for full time employees.

77. Define the term job specification/person specification. [2]

-It is a profile of the ideal candidate, which outlines expected qualification, skills and experience of the ideal candidate. It covers the knowledge, experience, physical characteristics, qualifications, age and personality of the candidate.

78. Give Henri Fayol's 14 principle's of management. [7]

-Division of work.

-Authority and responsibility.

-Discipline.

-Unit of command.

-Unit of direction.

-Subordination of individual.

-Remuneration.

-Centralization.

-Order.

-Equity.

-Stability.

-Initiative.

-Esprit de corps.

-Span of control.

79. Give any four forms of resolving conflicts.   [4]

-Collaboration

-Compromise

-Avoidance

-Accommodation

- Force

80. Give any four factors which affect motivation. [4]

-Pay salary.

-Security workers.

-Promotional prospects.

-Style of leadership.

-Working conditions.

-Nature of work.

81. What is meant by the term profit sharing in a business?   [2]

-It is a payment system which involves the distribution of the company's profits to workers so that workers will become more committed towards organizational success.

82. What are the effects of poor performance? [6]

-Deliberate absenteeism.

-Time wasting.

-Missing deadlines.

-Resisting change.

-Upsetting customers.

-Lack of commitment.

-Low output in quality and quantity.

83. Give any four examples of non financial benefits. [4]

-Certificate of appreciation.

-Worker of the year.

-Job design and its elements such as job rotation, job enlargement, job enrichment.

-Compressed work week.

-Job simplification.

-Worker involvement and participation.

-Employee Share Ownership Plans (ESOP).

84. Define the following terms in communication:

a. Encoding [2]

-This is when the sender of the message tries to establish mutuality of meaning with the receiver by choosing an appropriate channel / medium and symbol for communication.

b. Decoding [2]

-This refers to a situation where the receiver tries to deduce meaning by converting symbols into meanings.

c. Feedback [2]

-Refers to a situation when the receiver reports back to the sender / encoder about the message communicated.

85. How might workers actively resist change? [3]

-Minimum work or work to rule.

-Intentional errors.

-Sabotage.

-Slow down.

-Personal withdrawals.

-Absenteeism.

-Strike action.

86. Why do organizations carry out human resources planning? [6]

-To attract and retain staff.

-To fully utilize employees.

-To ensure that the employees receive all the training required for effective execution of tasks.

-To be able to anticipate and meet change in the demand / supply of labour.

-To ensure equal opportunities for promotion and development of staff readily available.

-To meet un-anticipated events such as resignation and death of employees.

-For succession planning.

87. Give any two types of collective bargaining. [2]

-Integrative bargaining.

-Distributive bargaining.

88. Define a strike action. [2]

-It is a temporary withholding of employees services from the employer for the purpose of getting greater gains.

89. Give any four unorganized of industrial action. [4]

-Theft.

-High labor turnover.

-Go slow.

-Faked illness.

-Destruction of property.

-Social loafing.

90. Justify the need for worker involvement and participation in organizations. [4]

-For employee empowerment.

-To improve productivity of work force.

-It improves the quality of products.

-It reduces labor turnover.

-To avoid resistance to change.

91. Give any two methods of change [2]

-Evolutionary change.

-Revolutionary change / transformational / quantum.

92. Give any five stages / levels of conflicts [5]

-Latent conflict.

-Perceived conflict.

-Felt conflict.

-Conflict manifestations.

-Conflict aftermath.

93. Give any four management functions [4]

-Planning.

-Organizing.

-Leading.

-Controlling.

94. Define the following terms [4]

a. RECRUITMENT

-It is a process of attracting a pool of qualified candidates to fill a vacant post.

b. SELECTION

-Choosing the job applicants who are suitable to fill the vacant positions.

95. What is the importance of communication to an organization. [4]

-It controls the behavior of employees by use of authority hierarchies and formal guidelines.

-Provides cheap and long distance communication.

-Offers unlimited potential for personal networking.

-Offers s platform for business transactions.

-Worldwide potential marketing.

-It opens up worldwide sources of information.

96. Outline the benefits a firm might gain from employing a personnel manager. [6]

-Analyzing job to gather information that can be used in selection.

-Training and development of employees' skills.

-Recruiting and selecting skilled employees.

-Administering systematic and fair programmes of compensation.

-Interacting with employee unions.

-Designing and administering employee benefits such as retirement and insurance programmes.

-Planning for organizational needs for various types of employees.

-Designing of jobs.

-Improving the motivation of work force.

97. How might management control absenteeism? [4]

-Careful job design to make work more satisfying.

-Increased participation in decision making.

-Allows employees flextime work.

-Job rotation makes work more interesting.

-Use of smaller working groups.

-Use an accurate rate of recording absenteeism.

-Employee counseling arrangements for persistence non attendance.

98. What is worker empowerment?   [2]

-Is the process of giving people power so that they can exercise power over their work.

99. Explain the benefits of empowerment [4]

Candidates should explain the following benefits:

-Speed of decision making.

-It releases the energy and creativity of the work force.

-It increases job satisfaction.

-It reduces the cost of supervision and control.

-Make better use of teams in the work force.

100. Explain three external sources of recruitment. [6]

Candidates should explain three of the following sources:

-Walk-ins.

-Employment agencies.

-Referrals.

-Professional associations.

101. What is the importance of job analysis? [4]

-It is used in manpower planning.

-It is used in recruitment and selection.

-It is used in establishing pay rates.

-Job analysis is also used in employee training and development.

- May be used in performance appraisal'

102. Explain any three factors which affect the selection decision [6]

Candidates should explain the following factors:

 -Nature of the organization.

-Size of the organization.

-Number of candidates for specific job.

-Trade unions.

-Government legislation.

MARKETING

1. Explain the meaning of marketing segmentation [2]

It is the subdivision of a heterogeneous market into homogeneous markets which are made up of customers with similar characteristics. The market can be segmented by age, sex, income, etc.

2. Why may business wish to segment markets for their products [4]

Candidates are expected to give the advantages of market segmentation only.

A business may segment its market because it:

- Leads to efficient allocation of resources
- Enables a firm to choose the market to serve
- Allows products tailor made to meet customer needs to be produced
- Enables firm to identify gaps or opportunities in the market
- Allows firm to develop appropriate marketing strategies suitable for each segment.

3. Outline how the market for soft drinks might be segmented in your country. [4]

Ways of segmenting the market might include:

- Age

- Occupation

- Income

- Use

- Geography

- Personality

4. What do you understand by the term mass marketing. [2]

It is a marketing strategy where a firm offers its products or services to the broader market without differentiating products to suit different customer segments. It is a blanket approach to marketing which try to satisfy the whole market with the same offering.

5. Define the term product life cycle. [3]

It refers to the stages that a product passes through from the time it was introduced into the market up until it is eliminated from the market. It shows the pattern of sales and profits of a product from introduction into the market up to its decline.

6. What are the differences between marketing and selling?   [4]

Students are expected to align their bases of differentiation so as to give a clear difference.

Marketing	Selling
It is a process of identifying, anticipating and satisfying customer needs profitably.	It is a process of disposing the product to the customers
It stresses on the needs of the buyers	It stresses on the needs of the sellers
Management is profit oriented	Management is sales volume oriented
Put emphasis on customer wants	Put emphasis on the product

7. **Evaluate the usefulness of price elasticity of demand when making pricing decisions. [4]**

Students are advised not to waste time defining price elasticity, they should dwell more on evaluating its significance in pricing decisions.

PED allows a firm to assess the responsiveness of its customers to price changes, hence if demand is elastic the firm will charge low prices in order to maximise revenue since customers will be more sensitive to price changes. Whereas if demand is inelastic it means that customers are less sensitive to price changes thus a firm can charge high prices to maximise revenue. However other factors like government policy should be considered by a firm when making a price because the government may put price floors or price ceilings which may render PED useless in price determination. In addition to the above the firm should also consider the level of competition in the industry because in a very competitive environment a firm may be forced to reduce prices even if demand is inelastic so as to remain competitive.

8. **What is forecasting [2]**

It is a process of predicting the future behaviour of a variable.

9. **Identify any three situations where forecasting may be useful. [3]**

Forecasting may be useful in:

Manpower planning

Investment appraisal

Budgeting

Market testing

Stock control

10. How might branding help in the successful marketing of a product. [3]

Candidates should show explicitly how branding might help in marketing of a product

- Differentiate product from those of competitors,

- Aid in product identification

- Act as a guarantee of quality

- Reduce price comparisons

- Create brand loyalty

- Add value to the product by making it more appealing.

- Can be used in market segmentation

11. Assess the usefulness of desk research. [4]

Answer should consider both merits and demerits of desk research.

Merits

- Less expensive and time consuming compared to primary research

- Prevent repetition of effort thus saving resources.

- Easier and quicker to establish trends as information is already in existence.

Demerits

- Information may be outdated and will fail to meet the firm's current needs

- Researchers have little control over quality of information.

- Problems of interpretation as the new researchers may not be aware of the context in which the information was gathered.

- Information may not be available especially for new and unique problems.

- Coverage may be inappropriate since it was gathered for other purposes.

12. State any three forecasting qualitative techniques

- Expert opinion (personal insights)

- Panel consensus

- Delphi method

13. List any four ways which a firm can use to extend the maturity phase of the product life cycle [4]

- Finding new markets for the product

- Finding new uses for the product

- Rejuvenating the product through rebranding and repackaging

- Developing a new range of accessories for the product

- Repositioning the product in another segment.

14. Outline three ways in which the production department is influenced by the activity of marketing. [3]

Marketing department will detect:

- Quality of raw materials to be used.

- Level of output to be produced for each segment

- Type of product to be produced for each segment

15. Under what circumstance might a full cost mark-up pricing method be the most appropriate one for a marketing manager to use? [4]

- It should be adopted when:

- Competition is very low

- Firm is producing a single product

- Demand is inelastic

- Demand for product is high.

16. Outline the factors that influence pricing decisions.

- Cost of production

- Level of competition

- Customer perception

- Nature of the economy

- Government policy

17. Discuss the factors that might influence the choice between desk and field research. [10]

Examples should be used to analyse and discuss each factor.

- Quality of researchers

- Availability of financial resources

- Nature of decision to be made

- Need for accuracy e.g. when introducing a new product.

18. Evaluate the usefulness of the result of market research to the marketing and production departments. **[15]**

Marketing department	Production department
Helps in pricing decision	Provide feedback about product design
Help in developing promotional mix	Provide feedback on product quality
Provide information on gaps and opportunities	Provide information for benchmarking
Help in market segmentation	Helps in determining product design
Help in developing distribution strategies and channels	Provides useful information for capacity planning and management
Help in fighting competition	
Provide information for positioning	

19. Explain the conditions necessary for a company to successfully charge different prices to various types of customers for the same product. [10]

Candidates should show knowledge and appreciation of price discrimination. Answer should consider the basis for the use of price discrimination e.g:

- The market should be segmented,

- The segments should have different price elasticity of demand,

- It should be impossible for customers in a low price segment to sale the product in a high price market segment.

- The discrimination should not drive customers away or cause resentment,

- There should be no opportunity for a competitor to under-price products that are being sold at high price.

20. Evaluate other various pricing methods that might be employed by firms and consider when each might be used. [15]

Answer should consider the following pricing methods and situations they can be effectively used.

- Price skimming

- Price penetration

- Mark up pricing

- Competitive pricing

- Perceived value pricing

21. Why do firms make new products?   [12]

- Replace declining markets

- Extend the life of declining products

- Spread risk

- Increase sales revenue and profitability

- In order to utilise extra capacity

- In order to fight competition

- To meet customer changing needs

22. 60% of newly introduced products fail. Discuss the reason for this.   [10]

- Misleading market research findings

- Poor timing

- Defects in the product

- Actions of competitors

- Poor marketing effort

- Unexpected increase in the cost of production.

- Inadequate market research findings.

23. State any three non probability sampling techniques

- Convinient sampling

- Multi stage sampling

- Quota sampling

24. Evaluate the contribution of advertising towards the marketing of goods and services   [12]

Advantages

- Provide useful information to the customers such as location, price and product benefits.

- It act as an aid to product identification especially when product brand colours are used as themes in the advert

- Help in product positioning

- Increases sales and profits

- Leads to impulse buying

- Reinforce brand emerge

- Encourage repeat purchase

Disadvantages

It increases costs of production and therefore increasing prices

It may increase customer expectations by misleading product performance.

It can be used by monopolies in maintaining market dominance.

25. Evaluate theusefulness of market segmentation to a manufacturer of clothes.   [13]

Merits

- Leads to efficient allocation of resources

- Enables a firm to choose the market to serve

- Allows products tailor made to meet customer needs to be produced

- Enables firm to identify gaps or opportunities in the market

- Allows firm to develop appropriate marketing strategies suitable for each segment.

- Help in product positioning

Demerits

- Increase cost of production due to product variation.

- It consumes both time and resources especially during marketing research

- It is difficult to conduct in small markets as they have a smaller number of customers, thus segmentation may further reduce the market making it less profitable.

26. Evaluate the factors that may influence a marketing manager's choice of distribution. [15]

- Nature of the product

- Nature of the market

- Financial strength

- Strategies used by competitors

- Stage on the product life cycle

- Positioning objective

27. Discuss the contribution of market research to a new tobacco processing firm. [12]

Merits

- Enables the firm to know both the market size and market location

- Enables the firm to identify opportunities and threats in the marketing environment

- Enables the firm to understand the strength and weaknesses of its competitors

- Helps in the development of appropriate marketing strategies

- Gives the firm a better understanding about its customer needs

- Allows the firm to know what motivates its customers

- Provides useful information for both market segmentation and market targeting.

However

- Process consumes resources, both time and finance

- The results from marketing research are only useful when they are interpreted correctly

- Data gathered is quickly outdated if the firm fail to act on it quickly.

- It is no guarantee of success as it depends on how the information gathered is used.

28. Evaluate the techniques that the firm might use to collect the market research data.   [13]

The answer should analyse both primary and secondary methods.

- Secondary methods include internal and external data sources

- Primary research data collection methods include: observations, experiments e.g. market testing, consumer panels, retail audits etc.

OPERATIONS AND PRODUCTION FUNCTION

1. A company manufactures product **x** and the following data is shown

Direct cost per unit	$70
Overheads	$50000
Current output	120000 units
Selling price	$140
Full capacity output	150000

From the above information calculate the company's capacity utilisation

Capacity utilization = current output over total [full] capacity x100

120000/150000x100= <u>80%</u>

2.State 2 ways in which a business may achieve added value. [2]

- promoting a product

- branding

- packaging

- exclusive and luxurious retail environment

- cost reduction

- product redesign

3.Why is added value important to a business. [4]

- allows firms to make their products more successful

- obtain a competitive advantage resulting in repeated purchase

- high added value products are less elastic and harder to copy

- a firm may be able to attain a unique selling price[USP]

- contributes to higher profitability

- improve corporate image

4.Define work study.   [2]

It refers to a series of techniques used to determine the most efficient use of labour in relation to other inputs in the production process.

or

It is the systematic analysis and measurement of a task in order to determine the best method and standard time of performing it.

5. Comment on the appropriateness of using a work study program by a timber manufacturing firm which is facing a high labour turnover problem.   [5]

NB :Reveal how a work study can be a motivational tool

Benefits

- estimate basis for incentives payments

- establish time that can be spent in each job to avoid overload

- improves utilization and safety of equipment and materials

- establishes easier methods of doing work

- Enhance efficiency and productivity

Demerits

- maybe time consuming

- Ignores differences between workers in terms of speed and talent.

- Mistrust by the employees may lead to resentment.

6. What are the advantages of line production to a company that manufactures soft drinks? [4]

- high productivity due to intensive use of machinery

- low unit cost as a result of mass production

- less industrial disputes as a result of more work being done by machines

- ability to satisfy fluctuations or increases in demand

- uses less skilled who are cheaper to pay

7. Mr Everjames is an old and experienced tailor who uses job production in making suits for his customers. Outline the possible advantages and disadvantages he is likely to encounter in his business. [5]

Advantages

- High motivation level as Mr Everjames is associated with final product.

- suits are made according to the customer specification hence less returns.

- production schedules can be prepared when customers arrive

- low cost of holding stock.

- has personal touch with customers

Disadvantages

- takes more time and efforts to design each suit

- High cost per suit due to short production run.

- customers dictate specifications which are varied hence greater need for flexibility

8. Explain any 4 factors of production. [4]

- land

- labour

- enterprise/entrepreneurship

- capital

NB: Students should explain briefly each factor to get marks.

9. Define the term productivity.   [2]

It is the measure of a ratio of a output to any of the firms inputs usually labour and capital.

10. Explain any 3 methods of raising productivity levels.[6]

- training of staffs

- purchase more technological advanced machine

- motivate staff financially and non financially

- division of labour and specialisation

- more efficient management

11. Define capacity utilisation.   [2]

it is a process of forecasting demand and then deciding what resources will be needed to meet that demand.

12. Define the term cellular production.   [2]

it is a form of flow production where production takes place in self contained units called cells.

13. What are the qualitative and quantitative factors influencing the location of the plant.   [4]

Qualitative

- infrastructure

- management preferences

- state and public opinions

- environmental concerns

Quantitative

- site cost

- transport cost

- labour cost

- revenue generation considerations

14. Stock usually takes 3 forms .what are these?   [3]

- raw materials

- semi-finished goods/ work in progress

- finished products

15. Why do a business hold stocks.   [4]

- to allow for variations in supply

- to take advantages of bulk buying discounts

- to gain from anticipated price rise

- to reduce stock and cost

16. Define the following terms   [4]

a. **buffer stock** ---this is the minimum stock reserve.

b. **Lead time**---it is the time interval between placing an order and receiving the order.

17. Give any 4 examples of stock out cost.   [4]

- loss of sales

- High cost due to rush purchases

- loss of customer goodwill

- idle production resources

18. What is the economic order quantity? [2]

It is the optimum stock quantity that should be ordered so as to minimise the both cost of holding stock and re-ordering stock.

19. Give any 3 examples of stock holding cost. [3]

- Pilferage

- insurance and security cost

- handling cost

- warehouse cost

- cash tied up in goods

- Deterioration

20. Define the quality. [2]

This refers to the fitness for purpose and safety in use of a product.

21. Why do businesses want to control the quality of their products? [5]

- to meet customer expectations hence satisfaction

- to ensure that products operate as claimed

- to make sure that the products satisfy the health and safety standard

- for customer loyalty

- reduces /eliminate the scrap of finished goods.

- a high price premium could be charged thereby increasing profitability.

- Create a competitive advantage for the firm.

- it saves on cost associated with customer complaints.

22. Evaluate the relevance of bench making [5]

Advantages

- the organisation will identify and improve the areas of great importance

- Motivate workers by showing them what is possible.

- the business will compete globally

- Prevents a firm from lagging behind key rivals

However

- the cost of comparisons may not be recovered by the improvement obtained

- the process depends on obtaining relevant and up to date information if this is difficult to obtain, then the process will fail

- copying ideas of other firms discourages initiative and originality

23. Outline the factors which determine the following.

a. Re-order   [3]

   - the nature of the product

   - the rate at which goods are sold

   - the likely price movement of the product

   b. Minimum stock levels   [3]

- lag time in delivery

- rate of turnover of stocks

- storage costs

24. Explain "just in time" as a stock holding policy [2]

It is a system of stock management in which materials are scheduled to arrive exactly when they are needed on the production line.

25. Distinguish between quality control and quality assurance[2]

Quality control is the practice of checking the quality of a product by testing samples. It is an important part of the manufacturing process, **whereas,** quality assurance involves preventive measures to overcome quality problems by training employees about quality, good investments in machines and good workflow methods.

26. Job production is one method of production. State any other 2.   [2]

- project

- flow/continuous

- batch

27. Under what circumstances do you think job production would be the best method.   [2]

When the product is a single item to be made according to customer specifications.

28. Give any 4 factors that determine the choice of the production method.   [4]

- cost

- availability of raw material

- availability of suppliers

- level of demand

- reliability of suppliers

- qualifications of staff

- availability of personnel

- level of technology

29. Outline the benefits of the" just in time "technique in stock management.   [4]

- Enhance product quality

- space is freed from stocking inventories

- storage cost are lowered

- the firm is given greater flexibility in its cash flow and liquidity etc.

FINANCE FUNCTION

1) Define the following terms:

a) Venture capital   [2]

-it is the sale of equity to a wealthy individual or organization that is willing to invest in a company with high potential for growth, once the business is able to sustain its self the venture capitalist will remove his capital and reinvest it in another company with high potential for growth.

b) Overtrading   [2]

-it is rapid expansion of a firm with insufficient working capital to finance the growth.

c) Working Capital   [2]

-it is money used to finance the day to day operations of a business. In accounting it is calculated by subtracting current liabilities from current assets.

d) Gearing [2]

-it is the extent to which a firm is financed by borrowed capital. It is calculated by dividing debt capital by equity capital.

e) Leasing [2]

-it is a contract whereby the owner of an asset called the lessor allows another firm called the lessee to use his asset in return of a payment.

2) Show **4** differences between **debt finance** and **equity finance.**   [4]

Debt Finance	Equity Finance
Represents borrowed capital e.g. Debenture	Represents owner's capital e.g. Ordinary shares
Holder have no voting rights	Holder have voting rights
Increase gearing	Decrease gearing
Holder receives a fixed return on amount invested	Holder receives varying amounts depending on profits made
Debt have a maturity period	It has no maturity period since it is a permanent source of finance.

3) What is the importance of listing a firm on the stock exchange?   [3]

-makes it easier for the firm to raise capital through the issue of shares and debenture stock

-allows shareholders to transfer shares whenever they want.

-market the firm on an international scale thus giving it a global reach

-gives a firm a better status and reputation.

3) Comment on any 2 short term sources of finance [4]

-Debt factoring, allows a firm to quickly improve its liquidity by selling its debts to a factoring firm at a discount **However** it results in loss of revenue as the firm does not receive the whole amount.

-Bank overdraft allows a firm to over draw its current account; it allows flexibility as a firm can only withdrew the amount suitable for its current needs. **However** it is expensive as interest is charged on a daily basis on the amount overdrawn.

4) Evaluate **leasing** as a source of finance.   [4]

Advantages

-Reduces initial outlay as a firm is allowed to use an asset they cannot afford to purchase currently.

-Repairs and maintenance of the asset are provided by the owner of the asset

-Payments on lease are tax deductible/.

Disadvantages

-it is expensive in the long run

-owner may put restrictions on the use of the asset

Firm does not benefit from residual value.

5) **Outline 4 methods a firm can use to manage its trade receivables.   [4]**

-Debt factoring

-offer cash discounts to encourage prompt payment.

-Charge high interest on overdue accounts to discourage delays in payments

-Assess credit worthiness of customers before granting credit

-reduce debtor collection period

6) **Using examples distinguish between a money market and a capital market. [2]**

-Money market is a market for short term sources of finance such as bank overdraft whereas capital markets are for long term sources of finance such as debentures.

7) **Identify 4** internal sources of finance.   [2]

-retained profit

-sale of surplus assets

-personal savings

-rights issue (issue of shares to existing shareholders)

8) Outline the factors that a firm considers when considering choice of finance. [4]

-amount required

-purpose of finance

-risk involved

-gearing ratio

-availability of sources of finance

-effect on control

9) Explain 3 ways a firm may use to improve its cash flow. [3]

-issue ordinary shares

-issue debentures

-debt factoring

-sale of surplus fixed assets

Sale and lease back

10) Explain 2 merits and 2 demerits of a debenture as a source of finance. [4]

Merits

-interest on debenture is tax deductible

-does not dilute power and dividends

Demerits

-increase gearing of the firm thus making it difficult for the firm to borrow in the future

-failure to service the debt may result in forced liquidation by creditors.

11) **Show 4 differences between profitability and liquidity. [4]**

Profitability	Liquidity
Measures performance by subtracting revenue from cost incurred	Measures the ability of a firm to easily convert its assets into cash
Profit is calculated on an accrual basis	It is calculated on a cash basis
It considers both cash and non-cash items	Considers only cash items
It is interpreted by profitability ratios such as ROCE	It is interpreted by liquidity ratios such as acid test ratio

12) **Assess the significance of high gearing to shareholders. [4]**

When profits are rising it enables shareholders to enjoy a higher return on their investments. Secondly firm raise more capital without diluting equity. **However** it reduces profits available to pay ordinary dividends in times of decreasing profits. In addition it reduces a firm's control over assets pledged as collateral on debt.

14) Outline the cost of granting credit. [3]

-cost of assessing credit worthiness of customers

-Bad debts

-loss of revenue through discounts for prompt payments

-opportunity cost of cash tied up in debts.

15) Outline cost of not granting credit.   [2]

-loss of sales

-loss of customer goodwill

16) Define the term cash equivalents.   [2]

-It refers to any short term investment that can be converted into cash without notice.

17) Why does a business need finance?   [4]

-to finance day to day operations (working capital purposes.)

-to develop new products.

-for expansion e.g. entering new markets.

-To upgrade plant and machinery.

18) Outline the risk associated with delaying payment of creditors. [4]

-loss of cash discounts

-risks of legal action

-interest on overdue

-Risks of losing suppliers

-loss of reputation

19) Assess the significance of sale of equity. [4]

It lowers gearing thus making future borrowing easier. Secondly there is no obligation to pay dividends hence they are only paid when there is a profit. Also there is no collateral required to access the finance. **However** there is dilution of control as well as dividends. Secondly it may be a costly way of raising finance especially if a prospectus is issued.

20) What are the functions of the stock exchange? [4]

-list and delist companies

-allows public limited companies to raise capital through the issue of shares and debenture stocks

-allows government to raise finance through the issue of treasury bills.

-it is an index used to measure economic performance of a country

---
THE END IS ONLY THE BEGINNING.

About The Author.

Solomon .T. Mbaimbai, is a business scientist, innovator, consultant and successful entrepreneur. He is a multi skilled young man with vast knowledge and experience in a variety of business related areas which include marketing, performance management, change management, organizational behaviour, industrial relations, economics, accounting, finance, innovation, technopreneurship, technovation, e-business, entrepreneurship, project management, business intelligence, and consumer and buyer behaviour. Currently he is the President of creative partners (pvt) Ltd and one connect media group. He is also the co-founder and general manager of Rotterview group of Schools and Realside College. Mbaimbai is also a passionate educationist with vast experience and knowledge in teaching accounting and business studies at both academic and professional level.

www.ingramcontent.com/pod-product-compliance
Lightning Source LLC
Chambersburg PA
CBHW051323220526
45468CB00004B/1474